Travels *with* Stanley

Travels *with* Stanley

by The Keepers of the Cup

TRIUMPH
BOOKS

Library of Congress Control Number: 2007902805

First published in Canada by Fenn Publishing Company

All images contained in this book are property of the Hockey Hall of Fame, and were taken by *The Keepers of the Cup*.

This book is available in quantity at special discounts for your group or organization. For further information, contact:

Triumph Books
542 South Dearborn Street
Suite 750
Chicago, Illinois 60605
(312) 939-3330
Fax (312) 663-3557

Printed in Canada
ISBN: 978-1-60078-048-6
Design by: First Image

Contents

Foreword

It was back in the early 1890's that through the efforts of his hockey-mad sons and daughter, Lord Frederick Stanley, Canada's sixth Governor General, got the idea to donate a trophy to the fledgling sport of hockey.

In 1893, the legend of the Stanley Cup began, with the Montreal Amateur Athletic Association being crowned the first winners. Although its official name is the Dominion Hockey Challenge Cup, the Stanley Cup, as it has always been called, is creating hockey history every day and everywhere it goes.

As the popularity of the game grew, so did the Stanley Cup itself. What started as seven inches in height is now closer to thirty-six inches. And although the Stanley Cup today weighs approximately thirty-five pounds, to those who have lifted it, it is virtually weightless.

The tradition of the on-ice celebration has grown organically through the years. In the early 1950's, Ted Lindsay startled onlookers by grabbing the Stanley Cup and hoisting it over his head out of sheer excitement. Thirty years later, to the delight of everyone watching, Wayne Gretzky skated around the ice with the Cup and then, spontaneously, handed it off to teammates so they too could enjoy the feeling. Today, with the red carpet treatment, the Keepers of the Cup and, of course, Commissioner Gary Bettman handing the championship trophy to an excited captain, the story continues to grow.

Over the years, the Stanley Cup has been dropped, left behind, forgotten, used as a planter and, of course, been the focus of team celebrations. The Bruins took the Cup for a joyride through the streets of Boston in the early '70's, and Lord Stanley's legacy

Travels With Stanley

NHL president Clarence Campbell
congratulates the winner of that
year's Stanley Cup final.

John Ziegler, NHL president,
greets the Stanley Cup champion
Edmonton Oilers in 1990.

practically lived in New York and Edmonton in the summers during the Islanders' and Oilers' dynasties.

The Penguins had well-known celebrations with the Cup in the early 1990's. Then, in 1993, the centennial of the Stanley Cup, there was no better team to win it than the Montreal Canadiens, returning the Cup to the city where the first celebration took place one hundred years earlier. The Canadiens toured the Cup around the province of Quebec, promoting the victory, the sport and, of course, the legend of the Cup. That year, it made some stops outside the borders of Quebec as well, including Vermont and Ontario.

Then, on a warm June night in downtown New York in 1994, the tradition of the Stanley Cup changed instantly, as a booming voice over the PA system stated: "Ladies and gentleman, the Stanley Cup!" Almost 20,000 people jammed into Madison Square Garden in New York, as well as eyes all around the globe watching on television, patiently waited for what seemed like an eternity; a moment that was fifty-four years in the making. Two members of the Hockey Hall of Fame staff walked out dressed in white shirts, ties and Hall of Fame blazers, each wearing white gloves, carrying the Stanley Cup. The Keepers of the Cup were officially born.

After a summer of excitement around New York and across North America, a new chapter in Stanley Cup celebrations was born. During the 1994-95 season, through the efforts of Commissioner Bettman, Bernadette Mansur and the staff of the National Hockey League along with Stanley Cup trustees and a staff member of the Hockey Hall of Fame, the decision was made to begin a new tradition. The team, including players, coaches and staff, would have the opportunity to celebrate personally with Lord Stanley. In 1995, each member of the winning team was given the chance to take the Stanley Cup home and celebrate with family and friends, neighbours, first coaches, former teammates or anyone else they wished.

Travels With Stanley

Hockey Hall of Fame curator
Maurice 'Lefty' Reid carries the
Stanley Cup out to centre ice,
ready for presentation.

The triumphant Montreal Canadiens
accept the Stanley Cup from NHL
commissioner Gary Bettman in 1993.

Mark Messier readies to hoist the
Stanley Cup for the sixth time when
his New York Rangers captured the
Cup in 1994.

Since then, every place the Stanley Cup has traveled, so too has a 'Cup Keeper.' Celebrations have taken place all across Canada and the United States and across the ocean to Russia, Siberia, Ukraine, Belarus, Sweden, Finland, Czech Republic, Slovakia and Switzerland.

Special note must be made of the Stanley Cup Trustees, the two men who, since Lord Stanley first donated the great trophy to hockey, have overseen and approved all activities associated with the Stanley Cup. The first two, Phillip Dansken Ross and John Sweetland, set the standard for ensuring the fair and reverent treatment of the Stanley Cup. Today, Scotty Morrison and Brian O'Neill, the current Trustees of the Stanley Cup, oversee and approve all movement of the world's greatest trophy.

Today, with hockey being played in more than sixty-five countries around the globe, and with every player who has ever donned a pair of skates and grabbed a hockey stick having dreamed of playing in the greatest league in the world, the National Hockey League, and imagined hoisting the Stanley Cup over their heads and enjoying the chance to bring home the Stanley Cup, the dream and the stories continue.

Hopefully, on the pages to follow, you will enjoy the photographs and stories that have taken place during some of the trips with the Stanley Cup. And maybe, just maybe, one day we'll stop by your hometown so you, like us, can be fortunate enough to take part in one of the adventures in our travels with Stanley.

The Keepers of the Cup, 2007

Travels With Stanley

Keepers Of The Cup

The Stanley Cup is always accompanied by a handler — one of several who rotate — supplied by the Hockey Hall of Fame. On the surface, being 'keeper of the Cup' is an incredible job, but underneath the shiny veneer are many sleepless nights, grabbing meals on the run, racing through airports to make yet another connecting flight, and extended travel time away from family and friends. Would we trade the opportunity for any other job in the world?

"No way!"

Philip Pritchard

Exactly what does the person who accompanies the Stanley Cup do? If you have seen MasterCard's award-winning 'Priceless' commercial featuring the Stanley Cup and Phil Pritchard, you get a pretty good idea — wherever the Cup goes, the keeper goes. Phil Pritchard is the Vice President of the Resource Centre and Curator of the Hockey Hall of Fame. Born in Oakville, Ontario, Phil's own hockey career began later than that of most Canadian boys. After playing road hockey with his pals for a number of years, he was finally able to convince his British-born Mom and Dad to register him for ice hockey at 13 years of age. Pritchard had discovered his passion, and now not only works in the hockey industry, but plays ice hockey and ball hockey several times a week all year round.

Phil began working at the Hockey Hall of Fame in September 1988. Less than a month later, he was first entrusted with the Stanley Cup, taking it to the annual banquet for the Newmarket Minor Hockey Association. Since then, Phil has been around the world, traveling more than a hundred days each year with hockey's most cherished prize.

Travels With Stanley

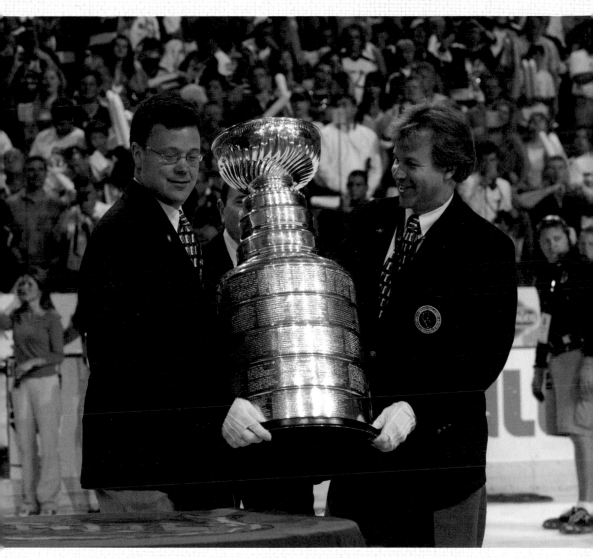

Craig Campbell (left) and Phil Pritchard carry the Stanley
Cup down the red carpet to centre ice and place it on the
skirted table, ready for the formal Cup presentation.

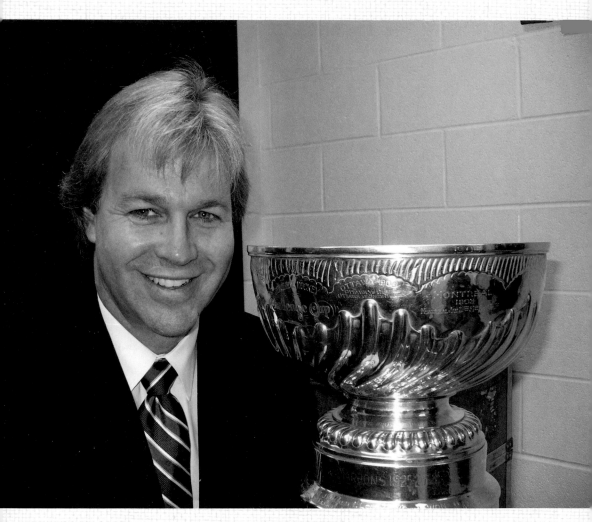

The Stanley Cup poses beside its
frequent traveling companion, Phil
Pritchard, prior to being escorted
to a presentation at centre ice.

It is near impossible for Phil Pritchard to isolate a single trip with the Stanley Cup that was more meaningful than the others, but he does show a genuine enthusiasm for the Stanley Cup's first trip to Russia. "After the Red Wings won the Cup in 1997, plans were made for Igor Larionov, Slava Kozlov and Viacheslav Fetisov to take the Stanley Cup to Russia for the first time. It was a rainy, dreary day, but when we arrived at Moscow's Sheremetyevo Airport, there were thousands of people waiting patiently behind guards and a chainlink fence to catch a glimpse of the Stanley Cup as it made its first visit to Russia. Fetisov walked the Cup over to the fence, and people stuck their fingers through it to touch the Cup. It was absolutely amazing!"

Pritchard has never lost his boyhood excitement for hockey or for the Stanley Cup. "In today's world, it is wonderful to be able to do something that makes people smile," he states. "Whether it is a visit to a player's hometown or taking the Stanley Cup to Sick Children's Hospital, everyone has a special place in their heart for the Stanley Cup!"

Craig Campbell

Like so many young boys, Craig Campbell's hockey dreams began while playing road hockey on the streets near his Scarborough, Ontario home. From the roads and a tennis ball, Craig graduated to ice and pucks by the age of six, and after a year of playing forward, exercised his fascination with goaltenders by asking if he could strap on the pads belonging to his brother's friend. A career was born, and to this day, Craig still plays goal in a recreational hockey league.

Campbell joined the Hall of Fame in June 1991, hired to organize the famous Imperial Oil/Turofsky photo collection. Since 1998, Craig and Phil have been the gloved caretakers who carry Lord Stanley's magnificent trophy out onto the ice for the NHL commissioner to present to the captain of the winning team. Campbell actually

Travels With Stanley

got a jumpstart on that annual ritual in 1993. During the Stanley Cup's one hundred-year anniversary, Craig was designated to take Lord Stanley's legacy to Montreal for Game 5 of that year's final. When the Canadiens won the game, and thus the Cup, Craig carried the trophy to the edge of the ice surface, surrendering the Cup to Lanny McDonald, Henri Richard and Billy Smith, who had been appointed Ambassadors of the Stanley Cup that year. The ambassadors then completed the trophy's journey to centre ice to present to the victorious Montreal Canadiens.

A memorable trip to Kenora, Ontario, the smallest town ever to lay claim to a Stanley Cup championship, doing so in 1907, is just one of many highlights from which Craig collects terrific memories. "Any time you travel with the Stanley Cup is a great honour and a great responsibility," states Campbell. "Everywhere you travel with the Cup, you're surrounded by happiness. That's the best thing!"

Mike Bolt

Mike Bolt spends as much time in the air as any transcontinental business executive. Yet, year in and year out, Mike embraces the busy itineraries and cheerfully accompanies the Stanley Cup. "Every year, the travel schedules seem to get more hectic," he admits.

Mike was born, raised and played organized hockey in the Leaside neighbourhood of Toronto. After managing his own cowboy boot and western wear store, Bolt joined the Hockey Hall of Fame in 1995, working on special events and as a guest services associate. His first adventure with the Stanley Cup was in 1997 at the downtown Toronto headquarters of the CBC, just a couple of blocks down the street from the Hockey Hall of Fame.

Mike's many memorable experiences with the Stanley Cup include the 24-hour period the Stanley Cup spent with Martin Brodeur during the Devils' netminder's

Dressed in requisite white gloves and smile, Craig Campbell poses with the Stanley Cup.

Mike Bolt pauses long enough to get a photograph with Andrew Ladd and the Stanley Cup.

summer of 2000 celebration. "Martin Brodeur really captured the dream of every kid growing up in Canada when it was his turn with the Cup. In 1995, he got all his childhood buddies together again to play road hockey, just like they used to when they were kids. On the same street, too. And just like years before, they played for the Stanley Cup — except this time, they really did!"

When the Devils won the Stanley Cup again, Brodeur got the same guys together and formed the same teams. He pulled out the same old battered net — it had been through many wars and was held together with duct tape. Martin later told me the irony of his street hockey days. When he was a kid, the neighbours used to yell at him to get off the street. Sometimes the cops would be called. And his Mom tried to get him to throw the net out. Now, twenty years later, here he is using the same net, the cops are there, though this time to block off the street so the guys can play and the neighbours are all out cheering them on. Hilarious!"

Mike Bolt sums up his role as the custodian who accompanies the Stanley Cup, saying, "Every day is a special day when you're with the guys who have won the Stanley Cup. It's been every kid's dream, and the players are no different than any of us; they are living that dream. Watching them with the Stanley Cup is amazing. That part of the job never gets old!"

Walt Neubrand

Walt Neubrand was born in Mississauga, Ontario and learned his hockey on the frozen surface of the Credit River. After graduating from university, Neubrand joined the Hockey Hall of Fame in 1995, working as a guest services associate. Two years later, he got his first taste of working with the Stanley Cup. It was following the Detroit Red Wings' 1997 Stanley Cup championship, and Walt was asked to accompany the Stanley Cup to Scotty Bowman's home in New York State.

Travels With Stanley

Being one of the Keepers of the Cup has additional advantages. While accompanying the Stanley Cup to the NHL All-Star Game in Tampa in 1999, Walt met Laura, a volunteer from Detroit. The two introduced themselves, and in 2003, Walt and Laura were married, settling into life in Hamilton, Ontario.

Spending so many days on the road with the Stanley Cup, Walt has seen the trophy in hundreds of different situations. "My favourite trip was taking the Stanley Cup to Rankin Inlet in Nunavut," explains Neubrand. "I love the wilderness, and this was an area above the tree line where there were no roads. People in the area are so passionate about hockey that some drove 250 miles by snowmobile just to see the Cup!"

During the summer, Walt is one of the Cup Keepers who travels from player to championship player, but during the hockey season, he returns to being an elementary school teacher in Mississauga, although he will occasionally travel with Lord Stanley's legacy through the school year. "Being the Cup Guy is a great job to have," Walt confirms. "As long as they allow me to do it, I'm honoured to accompany the greatest trophy in sports - the Stanley Cup."

Bill Wellman

Although a newcomer to attending the Stanley Cup, Bill Wellman is no rookie at the Hockey Hall of Fame, having joined the staff in 1993 just months before the legendary hockey attraction moved into its new location at Yonge and Front streets in Toronto. But Bill's ties to the Stanley Cup go back even further. "My grandparents lived not far from the old Hockey Hall of Fame when it was on the Exhibition Grounds, and each time we visited them, which was often, I begged my Mom and Dad to let me stop at the Hockey Hall of Fame, just for a minute, so I could look at the Stanley Cup," he smiles. "My grandfather, God rest his soul, used to say, 'One day, my boy, you'll be

Travels With Stanley

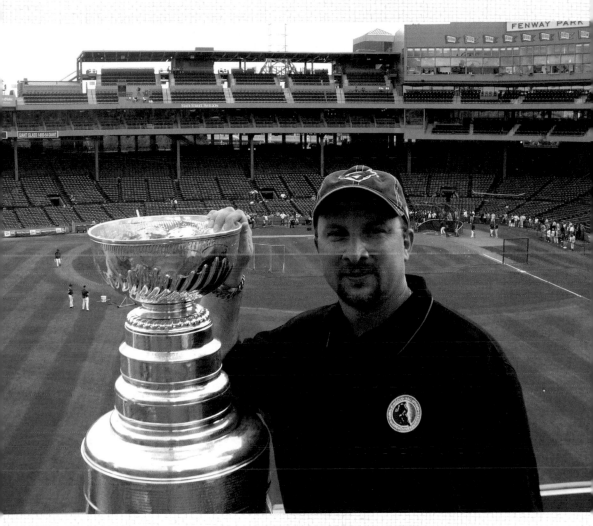

With baseball batting practice going
on behind him, Walt Neubrand
proudly poses with the Stanley Cup.

Bill Wellman accompanied the Stanley Cup to Europe in 2006, including a day with Josef Vasicek in the Czech Republic.

polishing that thing.'" Sure enough, one of Bill's proudest roles once he started at the Hall was to keep the Stanley Cup gleaming.

Toronto-born and raised, Wellman played hockey through his teens and had a real passion for the game when he was hired at the Hockey Hall of Fame. Bill occasionally traveled with various NHL trophies, including the Stanley Cup, but didn't join the ranks of Cup Keeper until the summer of 2006. "I can't begin to tell you how thrilling it was to travel to Europe with the Cup," Bill says, recalling a trip that took him to Switzerland, the Ukraine, Russia, the Czech Republic and Sweden. "To see the way people react to the Stanley Cup in countries that seldom see NHL hockey was mindboggling, and made me appreciate even more the impact this trophy has on people."

Wearing the requisite white gloves, above all else, Bill enjoyed hearing the adulation of hockey fans, cheering when he arrived at a destination with the Stanley Cup. "I know it wasn't for me, but deep down, I was just so proud to be bringing the Stanley Cup to fans who often had waited for hours, sometimes even a lifetime, to see the it. That's the greatest feeling in the world!"

Stanley Takes Up Space
Cape Canaveral, Florida

During the summer of 2004, the Stanley Cup visited the Kennedy Space Center in Florida at the invitation of NASA (the National Aeronautics and Space Administration) and the management of the Tampa Bay Lightning. The Cup traveled across the state of Florida for a unique look around the Kennedy Space Center, and sat perched in front of one of the launch pads. The launch pad, one of two at Complex 39, is located on Merritt Island, just north of Cape Canaveral, and was originally built in the 1960's to launch American astronauts on their historic journeys to the moon.

Stanley Makes Tracks

Weyburn, Saskatchewan

After visiting Jim McKenzie during the 2002 Stanley Cup tour with members of the champion New Jersey Devils, the Stanley Cup sat on railroad tracks that seem to go on forever just outside Weyburn, Saskatchewan. In fact, it took 4,406 miles (7,090 kilometres) of railroad track, stretching from Montreal, Quebec to Port Moody, British Columbia, to unite Canada in 1886. The last spike, which symbolically completed construction of the cross-Canada railroad, was driven into the ground by Sir Donald A. Smith, a director of the Canadian Pacific Railway (CPR) on November 7, 1885 at Craigellachie, British Columbia.

Stanley's Chilling with Willy

Porcupine Plain, Saskatchewan

During 'Hockey Day in Canada' in 2005, the Stanley Cup traveled to Porcupine Plain, Saskatchewan, the home of Kelly Chase, and visited the town's mascot, Quilly Willy. Porcupines come from the rodent family and usually weigh just over 20 pounds (9 kilograms). The front half of a porcupine's body is covered in long guard hairs, and the back half and tail are covered with more than 30,000 quills. Each quill is between one inch and two-and-a-half (2.5 to 6.5 centimetres) inches in length and has tiny barbs.

Stanley Goes Against The Grain

Davidson, Saskatchewan

En route to the celebration planned for Tampa Bay's Cory Sarich in 2004, the Stanley Cup sat amidst acres and acres of prime Canadian wheat on a Saskatchewan farm. Canada is one of the world's largest wheat suppliers, averaging 24.5 million tons each year. Although wheat is grown across Canada, most is grown in Canada's prairie provinces. Saskatchewan is the largest supplier, followed by Alberta and Manitoba.

Travels With Stanley

Stanley is all Shook Up

Memphis, Tennessee

In the spring of 2003, the Stanley Cup made a tour of Central Hockey League team locations, and through the efforts of the Memphis River Kings, made a pilgrimage to Graceland, the magnificent Memphis, Tennessee home of Elvis Presley. Elvis was one of the pioneers of rock and roll. In 1956, as rock and roll was finding its earliest fans, Elvis had five songs climb to the number one spot on the charts – 'Heartbreak Hotel', 'I Want You, I Need You, I Love You', 'Don't Be Cruel', 'Hound Dog' and 'Love Me Tender'.

Travels With Stanley

Stanley Goes to the Park
Algonquin Park, Ontario

The Stanley Cup traveled to Ontario's cottage country during 1999 as the special guest of several members of the Dallas Stars. The magnificent trophy visited Algonquin Provincial Park, a 7,725 square kilometre area (2,983 square miles) of Ontario wilderness made up of forests, lakes, streams and wildlife. Established in 1893, Algonquin Park straddles a very interesting spot, with coniferous forests typical of areas north of the park and deciduous forests typical of areas south of the park. Look carefully and you'll see black bears, beavers, white-tailed deer, moose, wolves, frogs, toads, turtles and snakes as well as smallmouth bass, yellow perch, northern pike, lake trout and walleye.

Welcome To The Valley
Blue Earth Mn

Stanley Dwarfed by Green Giant

Blue Earth, Minnesota

Following the 2004 NHL All-Star Game in St. Paul, Minnesota, the Stanley Cup was taken on a three-hour detour. Although the Stanley Cup looms large to the fortunate players who win it, it was dwarfed by the 55-foot tall (16.7 metres) Jolly Green Giant in Blue Earth, Minnesota. The Jolly Green Giant overlooks some of the richest farmland in the United States. Blue Earth is a town of only 4,000 residents, yet it is not only home to the statue of the Green Giant, but is also the birthplace of the ice cream sandwich. Ho! Ho! Ho!

Stanley and a Jersey

Asbury Park, New Jersey

The Stanley Cup sits on the Jersey Shore, a favourite vacation spot for over a century. From Long Branch at the top end to Cape May in the south, the Jersey Shore is comprised of a number of seaside resorts with fabulous boardwalks. Among the best known are Asbury Park, Spring Lake, Point Pleasant Beach, Ocean City and Wildwood. The New Jersey shoreline was a frequent stop for the Cup during the three years (1995, 2000 and 2003) it was won by the Devils.

Stanley Gets Scrubbed

Los Angeles, California

Every night, after the celebrations are over, the Keepers of the Cup have one final duty – to give the Stanley Cup a good scrub in preparation of the next celebration. After all, think of all those fans who have had the opportunity to touch the Stanley Cup and leave their mark on the game! The earliest bathtub discovered came from 1,000 BC and is a five-foot(1.5 metres) tub made out of hard pottery discovered on the island of Crete. It was the Romans between 500BC and 450AD who made daily bathing a ritual, most commonly using public baths.

Stanley Meets Lenin

Arkhangelsk, Russia

The icy waters of the White Sea splash the coastline and winters last close to 250 days in Arkhangelsk, a city in the north-west part of Russia. Originally named Novo-Kholmogory, in 1613, the city was renamed after the monastery of the Archangel Michael, which still exists. Among the incredible sculptures and monuments viewed by the Stanley Cup was this gigantic statue of Vladimir Lenin located in Petrovskiy Park in the heart of Arkhangelsk. Lenin headed the Soviet government from 1917 until he retired in 1922. In 2004, the Tampa Bay Lightning had a roster that included players from all over the world, which meant stops overseas, including Dmitry Afanasenkov's hometown in Russia's far north.

Stanley Meets Sandy

Atlantic City, New Jersey

With teams like the New Jersey Devils, Tampa Bay Lightning and Carolina Hurricanes located along the Atlantic Ocean, the beaches along the east coast became a regular stop for hockey celebrations. The Stanley Cup sits by its mirror image sculpted entirely of sand. The first person to have earned money creating a sand sculpture was Philip McCord, who on June 20, 1897, created out of sand on the beach at Atlantic City, New Jersey, a tragic scene of a drowned mother and baby. Those strolling along the famous boardwalk threw coins to the artist, who tucked them into his bowler hat. Within a few years, every block along the Atlantic City beach and boardwalk was occupied by an enterprising sand sculptor hoping to earn some spare change. On September 14, 1944, a hurricane demolished more than half of the boardwalk and wiped out most of the sand dunes at Atlantic City.

Travels With Stanley

Stanley Makes Waves

Lake Erie, Ontario

With the Detroit Red Wings having won the Stanley Cup three times over the past decade, the cottage of assistant coach Barry Smith has become a familiar stop for celebrations. Looking out as the sun calmly sets and the waves gently lap onto the shore, the Stanley Cup sits peering out at Lake Erie, the smallest of the five Great Lakes. Lake Superior is the largest, followed by Lake Michigan and Lake Huron. Lake Ontario is about the same size as Lake Erie, but holds about four times as much water due to its depth. Although not considered one of the Great Lakes, Lake St. Clair is part of the Great Lakes System, situated between Lake Erie and Lake Huron. The Great Lakes hold six quadrillion gallons of water, which is one-fifth of the world's fresh water supply.

Stanley Reveres the Rocket

Gatineau, Quebec

The Stanley Cup pays tribute to one of the NHL's greatest stars. After the grand opening of 'The Rocket' display at the Museum of Civilization, the Stanley Cup stopped for a photograph with a star who won the Cup on eight occasions. Through 18 NHL seasons, Maurice 'Rocket' Richard scored an incredible 544 goals and collected 965 points in 978 regular season games. 'The Rocket' was the first NHL player to score 50 goals in one season, accomplishing that feat in 1944-45. The Stanley Cup was won by Maurice Richard eight times, including five times in a row between 1956 and 1960. 'The Rocket' was elected to the Hockey Hall of Fame in 1961. When Richard died on May 27, 2000, thousands of fans lined the streets outside Notre Dame Basilica in Montreal where the funeral was held. On June 27, 2001, a bronze statue honouring Maurice 'Rocket' Richard was unveiled in Gatineau, Quebec's Parc Jacques Cartier. Today, the NHL player who scores the most goals in the regular season is awarded the Maurice 'Rocket' Richard Trophy.

Stanley Rides a Zamboni

Tampa, Florida

Now come on, be honest. Just like everyone dreams of winning the Stanley Cup, is there anyone who wouldn't love to ride on a Zamboni? Some of the ice resurfacing machines we see between periods at hockey games are known as Zambonis. Frank Zamboni moved to Southern California in 1922 and, with two family members, opened the Iceland Skating Rink in Paramount, California in 1940. At that time, it took over an hour to resurface the ice: a tractor pulled a scraper that shaved the surface of the ice. Then, several rink workers followed behind shoveling the ice shavings and spraying water over the ice's surface, then allowed the water to freeze. Frank Zamboni created a machine that made ice resurfacing much more efficient and a whole lot quicker!

Stanley's up to Par

Denver, Colorado

Although known as hockey's most cherished trophy, the Stanley Cup enjoys

other sports as well. Just like the game of hockey evolved from various stick

and ball games, so too did golf. Although a game similar to golf may have been

played earlier in Holland or Italy, the first reference to golf came in 1457 when

King James II of Scotland issued a ban on the game because it interrupted his

archers. The first written rules for golf were developed in Edinburgh, Scotland

in 1744. During the summer months, if players aren't training for the upcoming

season, they are golfing, and inevitably, the Cup ends up on golf courses all

across North America as part of Stanley Cup celebrations. This particular day of

golf was spent with Bob Hartley at an exclusive club outside Denver, Colorado.

Stanley Braces for a Race

Indianapolis, Indiana

What the Stanley Cup is to hockey, the Borg-Warner Trophy is to Indy Car racing. Each year, the winner of the Indianapolis 500 is presented with the Borg-Warner Trophy. First awarded in 1936, it was commissioned by the Borg-Warner Automotive Company. The trophy stands 64½ inches tall (164 centimetres) while the Stanley Cup is 35¼ inches in height (89.5 centimetres). The Borg-Warner Trophy weighs 150 pounds (68 kilograms) while Lord Stanley's Cup is 34½ pounds (15.5 kilograms). Whereas each player on the NHL's championship team gets his name engraved on the Stanley Cup, each winner of the Indianapolis 500 gets an image of their face added to the Borg-Warner Trophy. The Stanley Cup, when not on tour, is kept at the Hockey Hall of Fame while the Borg-Warner Trophy is permanently displayed at the Indianapolis Motor Speedway Hall of Fame Museum in Indianapolis, Indiana. In early 2002, the NHL held a media tour across the United States, and included a sneak peek at the Indianapolis 500, where racers and mechanics alike were fascinated by the Stanley Cup's legend.

Stanley's High Flight
Chicago, Illinois

"This is your captain speaking. We are cruising at an altitude of 41,000 feet. Sit back, relax and enjoy your flight along with our special visitor, the Stanley Cup." In order to arrive at destinations, the Stanley Cup often travels by plane. At times, the airlines allow the Cup to travel like a passenger, but otherwise, they find a special spot underneath with the baggage, On December 17, 1903, Orville and Wilbur Wright made the first powered flight when their glider 'The Flyer' made a 12-second flight from sand dunes at Kill Devil Hills, four miles (6.4 kilometres) south of Kitty Hawk, North Carolina. J.A.D. McCurdy made the first powered flight in Canada when he flew a bi-plane called 'Silver Dart' on Cape Breton Island at Baddeck, Nova Scotia on February 23, 1909. "Now, please return your tabletop to its upright position, fasten your seatbelt and prepare for arrival."

Travels With Stanley

Stanley's Statue

Vancouver, British Columbia

The Stanley Cup visits its donator in Vancouver, British Columbia. Lord Frederick Arthur Stanley was Canada's Governor General between 1888 and 1893. Lord Stanley traveled extensively during his time in Canada. In 1889, the Governor General visited western Canada. While in Vancouver, Lord Stanley dedicated a 1,000-acre park named in his honour, stating that the natural beauty of Stanley Park was "…to the use and enjoyment of people of all colours, creeds and customs for all time." In 1893, Lord Stanley left another legacy of his time as Governor General – he donated the Dominion Hockey Challenge Cup, now better known as the Stanley Cup.

Stanley Stands Proud

Montreal, Quebec

When many people think of Canada, they visualize the image of a 'Mountie', wearing a crimson red jacket and broad-brimmed Stetson hat. Like the Stanley Cup, a Mountie is something specific to Canada's cultural identity. Mounties are members of the Royal Canadian Mounted Police, Canada's national police force. One of their most popular activities is the Musical Ride, a proud tradition of the RCMP since it was first performed in 1887 in Regina, Saskatchewan. Today, the Musical Ride is made up of 32 RCMP officers mounted on 32 horses performing a series of intricate drills choreographed to music. During Martin Lapointe's 1998 Stanley Cup party, the Stanley Cup was taken to a training area used by the RCMP just outside of Montreal.

Stanley's Football Friend
Edmonton, Alberta

In November 2003, the City of Edmonton hosted the Heritage Classic Game, where the NHL played a regular season game outdoors for the first time. Both the Stanley Cup and its sporting sister, the Grey Cup, were present in the City of Champions for that contest. Both extraordinary trophies were donated for achievement in sport by Governors General of Canada. The Grey Cup, donated in 1909 for the senior football championship of Canada, was donated by Lord Grey, the ninth Governor General of Canada. The Stanley Cup was donated in 1893 for the amateur hockey championship of Canada by Lord Stanley, Canada's sixth Governor General.

Travels With Stanley

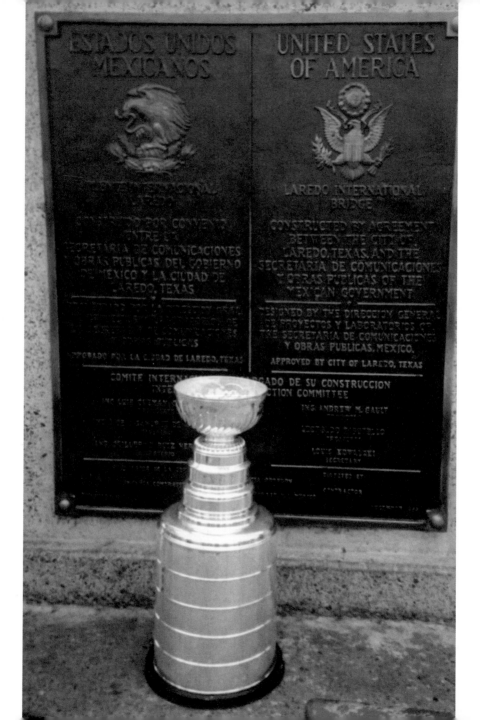

Stanley Straddles the Border

Laredo, Texas/Nuevo Laredo, Tamaulipas

In 2006, Rio Grande, Texas played host to the Central Hockey League's All-Star Game. Right across the street was the Mexican border. The international border that runs between the United States and Mexico extends 3,141 kilometres (1,952 miles) and follows the middle of the river known as the Rio Grande, which, in Mexico, is called the Rio Bravo. The Stanley Cup straddles the cities of Laredo in the state of Texas and Nuevo Laredo in the state of Tamaulipas. Laredo is home to 200,000 residents; Nuevo Laredo has 400,000 citizens. This was the first time the Stanley Cup had visited Mexico.

Stanley Salutes the President
Washington, D.C.

Each year, when an American-based team wins the Stanley Cup, the champions get invited by the President of the United States to visit the White House. Construction on the White House, the official residence of the President of the United States, began in 1792 but was not completed until 1800. John Adams was the first president to live in the White House. The exterior of the building at 1600 Pennsylvania Avenue was painted white from its beginning, but the term White House wasn't used officially until 1901 when President Theodore Roosevelt included the term on his presidential stationery. There are 132 rooms, including 35 bathrooms, contained in the six storeys of the White House.

Stanley Pays Tribute to a King

Memphis, Tennessee

Dr. Martin Luther King, one of the world's foremost civil rights leaders, was shot to death on April 4, 1968 while standing on the balcony of the Lorraine Motel in Memphis, Tennessee. This motel, left intact since the shot rang out in the Memphis sky, now serves as the National Civil Rights Museum, and during an event with the Memphis River Kings of the Central Hockey League, the Stanley Cup visited in 2004. The band U2 paid tribute to Martin Luther King Jr. in their song 'Pride (In the Name of Love)'. Martin Luther King Day is celebrated in the United States each year on the third Monday in January. The Nobel Peace Prize recipient in 1964 left an enormous legacy during his abbreviated life. In the words of his "I Have a Dream" speech, delivered August 28, 1963, "I have a dream that my four children will one day live in a nation where they will not be judged by the colour of their skin but by the content of their character!'"

Travels With Stanley

Stanley and Sun

Memphis, Tennessee

The Stanley Cup went looking for the birthplace of rock and roll and discovered the Sun Records recording studio. In 1952, Sam Phillips launched a record company in a former radiator shop at 706 Union Avenue in Memphis, Tennessee. He named it Sun Records and began to record some of the world's most exciting young artists – Elvis Presley, Johnny Cash, Roy Orbison, Carl Perkins, Charlie Rich and Jerry Lee Lewis. The label recorded a new brand of music called rockabilly. "Rocket 88," considered by some historians to be the first rock and roll song, was recorded at Sun Records by Jackie Brenston and his Delta Cats. Later, when Elvis sang "That's All Right (Mama)", Carl Perkins recorded "Blue Suede Shoes" and Jerry Lee Lewis released "Great Balls Of Fire" and "Whole Lotta Shakin' Goin' On," Sun Records not only found its place on the musical map but confirmed its spot in music history. In 2004, while visiting the CHL's Memphis River Kings, the Stanley Cup stopped by the legendary studio.

Travels With Stanley

Stanley and the Prairie Dog

Val Marie, Saskatchewan

Although millions of prairie dogs once inhabited the plains and grasslands of North America, today, their existence is relegated to specific areas, including the Val Marie area of southern Saskatchewan, the hometown of Hall of Fame star Bryan Trottier. Prairie dogs, so named because of their dog-like 'yips,' live in underground tunnels or burrows. These large rodents have sharp claws for digging and hibernate deep within their burrows during the winter. It has been discovered that prairie dogs are able to communicate with each other in a language that uses different sounds to identify various predators, allowing others in their prairie dog community to scamper away and disappear into their burrows.

Stanley Gazes at the Atlantic
Cape Spear, Newfoundland

While attending the 2004 World Under-17 Hockey Challenge in St. John's, Newfoundland, the Stanley Cup had the opportunity to sit on the rocks at Cape Spear, Newfoundland, gazing out towards Ireland, some 3,000 miles (4,828 kilometers) away across the Atlantic Ocean. A spit of land jutting out into the ocean, Cape Spear is found just a few kilometers away from St. John's and at 52 degrees west longitude, is the most easterly spot in Canada. Newfoundland, which joined Canada in 1949, was first claimed by explorer John Cabot in 1497, who claimed the 'new found land' for King Henry VII of England. Cape Spear, as the most easterly Canadian location, is 9,306 kilometres (5,780 miles) away from the most westerly spot — Mount St. Elias in the Yukon Territory (141 degrees west longitude).

Travels With Stanley

Stanley Hails a Hero

Thunder Bay, Ontario

During the summer following the locked-out season, the Stanley Cup visited a number of former Stanley Cup champions in order to give them a long overdue celebration with the Cup. That summer of 2005, after visiting Steve Black, Dave Gatherum and Benny Woit in Thunder Bay, the Stanley Cup paid tribute to a Canadian hero. Terry Fox was born in Winnipeg, Manitoba on July 28, 1958, but raised in Port Coquitlam, British Columbia. In 1977, just 18 years of age, Terry had his right leg amputated above the knee after being diagnosed with bone cancer. While in the hospital, he was inspired to run across Canada in order to raise money for cancer research. Terry began his 'Marathon of Hope' in St. John's, Newfoundland on April 12, 1980. Although he received little attention at the beginning, enthusiasm for his cross-Canada run grew and the money collected along the way began to mount. He ran 42 kilometres (26 miles) each day through the Atlantic provinces, Quebec and Ontario, however, on September 1, 1980, after 5,373 kilometres (3,339 miles) and 143 days, Terry was forced to halt the marathon outside Thunder Bay, Ontario. The cancer had returned. Although the Marathon of Hope lasted less than five months, the entire country mourned the death of Terry Fox on June 28, 1981. The heroic Canadian was gone but his legacy had just begun. The Terry Fox Scenic Lookout, on which the Stanley Cup is perched, was constructed just 12 kilometres (7 miles) from where Terry was forced to abandon his dream, and was dedicated on June 26, 1982.

Travels With Stanley

Stanley Put on Ice

Rankin Inlet, Nunavut

On a tour of Canada's north, the Stanley Cup stopped in Rankin Inlet and discovered that in parts of Nunavut, igloos are a way of life when hunting or fishing. Much warmer than a tent, an igloo is constructed of blocks of snow, and is ideally suited as temporary lodging for two or three people (or the Stanley Cup). The word "igloo" is Inukitut for "house." Nunavut, which is an Inukitut word meaning "our land," was formed April 1, 1999 and covers one-fifth of Canada's total land mass to the west of Hudson Bay and extending north to the Arctic Circle.

Stanley and the Dinosaur

Milk River, Alberta

While returning from a trip to Montana, the Stanley Cup visited Milk River, Alberta, the home of John MacMillan, a Cup winner with the Toronto Maple Leafs in 1962 and 1963. There, in southern Alberta, they discovered a unique photo opportunity. The Tyrannosaurus Rex existed during the Cretaceous Period approximately 70 million years ago. It was a fierce beast, standing 20 feet tall (6.1 metres), stretching 40 feet in length (12.2 metres)and weighing as much as 7 tons (7,100 kilograms). The T. Rex had a huge, muscular jaw that contained fifty to sixty piercing teeth. (Gulp!) Thank goodness for the Stanley Cup that the Tyrannosaurus Rex was a meat eater and would have little interest in chewing a silver trophy.

Stanley Meets a Moose

Moose Jaw, Saskatchewan

Mac the Moose welcomes visitors, like the Stanley Cup, to Moose Jaw, Saskatchewan during a cross-Canadian trip promoting the 2002 Stanley Cup playoffs. A moose, whose scientific name is 'alces alces,' is a member of the deer family. In spite of its fierce appearance, which includes a height to the shoulders of over 2.25 meters (7.4 feet), a length of 2.75 meters (over 9 feet) and weight that can exceed 630 kilograms (1390 pounds) as well as antlers that can grow to 2 meters (6¾ feet) in width, is actually a vegetarian. Ironically, the City of Moose Jaw's name likely has nothing to do with the mammal. The city's name comes from the Cree word "moosegaw," which means "warm breezes."

Stanley Takes a Bow

Vancouver, British Columbia

Because player celebrations most often take place during the summer, Stanley Cup parties are often held on the water, as many players rent private cruise ships for the enjoyment of their families and friends. On this date, the Stanley Cup was a guest of the Colorado Avalanche, cruising the British Columbia coast. The Stanley Cup looks out over the ocean and just like Leonardo DiCaprio in 'Titanic', seems to be shouting, "I'm the king of the world!" The 'Titanic' left England on its maiden voyage April 14, 1912, heading to the United States with 2,229 passengers and crew members when, late that night, it struck an iceberg. The 'unsinkable' ship was damaged so severely that it broke in two and sank to its watery grave at a spot about 1,000 miles (1,610 kilometres) east of Boston, Massachusetts and 375 miles (603 kilometres) southeast of St. John's, Newfoundland. "Slowly and almost majestically, the immense stern reared itself up, with propellers and rudders clearing the water, till at last, she assumed the exact perpendicular," wrote a survivor who watched the ship's tortuous death. "Then, with an ever-quickening glide, she slid beneath the water of the cold Atlantic. Like a prayer as she disappeared, the words were breathed, 'She's gone.'" Only 705 people were rescued as the 'Titanic' found a permanent resting spot 12,500 feet (3,810 metres) below the surface of the Atlantic Ocean.

Travels With Stanley

Stanley Chills with the Champions

Raleigh, North Carolina

Through the centuries, champagne has become known as the drink of champions. With every Stanley Cup championship win comes the popping of corks and celebrations with 'the bubbly,' as in this celebration being held in Raleigh, North Carolina by the scouts of the reigning Stanley Cup champion Tampa Bay Lightning following the 2004 NHL Entry Draft. True champagne is a sparkling wine produced exclusively in the Champagne region of northeastern France. Champagne comes in a variety of sizes: a bottle is 25.4 fluid ounces, a magnum is 50.8 fluid ounces, a jereboam is 147 fluid ounces, a methuselah is 196 fluid ounces, a salmanazar is a hefty 304.8 fluid ounces and a nebuchadnezzar, as difficult to pronounce as it is to lift, is 508 fluid ounces, or the equivalent of 20 bottles.

Stanley Presents...

Detroit, Michigan

Christmas is a very special time of year for the Stanley Cup; a time of celebration and for gift-giving. During a media tour of the NHL's playoff tours, a display was set up suggesting the Stanley Cup as the ultimate Christmas gift for any hockey player. The idea of a magical figure distributing gifts to children is traced to a fourth century bishop from Asia Minor named Saint Nicholas of Bari. The Dutch brought the feast of Sinterklaas to North America in the nineteenth century, and the name of the generous gift-bearing figure was altered to Santa Claus. In various parts of the world, the figure known as Santa Claus is referred to by a variety of names. Santa Claus is known as Father Christmas, Kris Kringle or Saint Nick in different English-speaking countries. In French-speaking homes, he is called Pere Noel. In parts of China, he's Sheng Dan Lau Ren. In Japan, Hoteisho. German children look forward to a visit from Wiehnachtsmann. In Russia, Ded Moroz (Grandfather Frost) brings gifts. Swiety Mikolaj brings gifts to Polish children and Ganesha to children from India. In Finland, Joulupukki visits while in Sweden, it's Jultomten. Italians celebrate with Babbo Natale and Greeks with Hagios Nikolaos. All in all, the idea of giving gifts has turned into a delightful custom in most countries around the world.

Travels With Stanley

Stanley Goes to Sweden

Pitea, Sweden

More than 9 million citizens call Sweden home. The beautiful country is 450,000 square kilometers (174,000 square miles) in size, of which more than half is still covered in forest. Mountains make up 11% of Sweden while rivers comprise 9%. Stockholm is the capital of Sweden. The Swedish flag, hovering here above the Stanley Cup, has been flown since at least the 1600's. June 6, 1916 was designated as Swedish Flag Day, which became Sweden's National Day in 1983. June 6 holds special significance to Swedish citizens – it's the date Gustav Vasa was elected Sweden's king in 1523, and also the date Sweden adopted its new constitution in 1809. As a member of the Detroit Red Wings, Tomas Holmstrom has enjoyed three Stanley Cup parties in his hometown of Pitea, in the northern part of Sweden.

Stanley Goes to the Ballgame
Seattle, Washington

Baseball, just like hockey, was not invented in one day but evolved from a series of games. Although for decades, the story of Abner Doubleday inventing baseball in 1839 has been circulated, baseball's roots have been traced back to the English games of rounders, goal ball and old cat, the Dutch game of stool ball and an American game called town ball. The earliest reference to baseball comes from a 1791 bylaw for a small Massachusetts town called Pittsfield, which was instituted to protect the windows in the new town hall by prohibiting anyone from playing "baseball" within 80 yards (73 metres) of the building. Today, Major League Baseball is comprised of thirty franchises; sixteen in the National League and fourteen in the American League. The Stanley Cup sits on the first base line watching a game at Safeco Field in Seattle, Washington.

Stanley Rides an Elevator

Shaunavon, Saskatchewan

Agriculture dominated the prairie provinces of Canada from the 1870's until the 1960's, and the majestic grain elevators rising from the flat landscape came to symbolize rural life. The first grain elevators were erected in the 1870's and served as vertical warehouses, storing as much as 35,000 bushels of grain. More than 6,000 such buildings were constructed between 1870 and 1930, spaced approximately seven to eleven miles (11 to 18 kilometres) apart and, for ease of transportation, built along railway lines. Although quickly disappearing from the prairie landscape, approximately a thousand of these wonderful grain elevators still exist, and the Stanley Cup peers affectionately at grain elevators located in the Shaunavon, Saskatchewan, the home of Hayley Wickenheiser, during CBC's 'Hockey Day in Canada.'

Travels With Stanley

Stanley Flies Above the Clouds

Cleveland, Ohio

A helicopter is a most unique aircraft as, unlike any other mode of transportation, it is able to fly forwards, backwards, up, down or can hover motionless in the air. Although this makes it a most complicated craft to fly, a helicopter is ideal for accessing areas that no other vehicle, land or sky, can reach. The medical team of the New Jersey Devils' arranged for a helicopter tour of the Great Lakes during their day with the Stanley Cup. In 1907, a French aviator named Paul Cornu lifted an early helicopter into the air for a few seconds without assistance, but it wasn't until 1924 that a helicopter was able to remain sustained in flight, piloted by another French flying pioneer, Etienne Oehmichen. One of the earliest prototypes of the helicopter was designed in the late-1400's by inventor Leonardo daVinci. Regrettably, in DaVinci's vast wisdom, he never tried his hand at inventing hockey.

Travels With Stanley

Stanley Gets the Czech
Znojmo, Czech Republic

Following World War I, a country called Czechoslovakia was formed from the former Austro-Hungarian Empire. The country remained under Soviet authority, but when the USSR collapsed, Czechoslovakia attained its freedom through what is known as the 'Velvet Revolution.' On January 1, 1993, the country was divided into two national components: the Czech Republic and Slovakia. Today, the Czech Republic is home to 10,250,000 residents, who celebrate Czech Founding Day as a national holiday each October 28. The Stanley Cup visited Znojmo, Czech Republic in 2003 as the guest of Patrik Elias of the New Jersey Devils, where thousands of fans converged on the historic city to get a glimpse of the Stanley Cup.

Travels With Stanley

Stanley and the Needle

Seattle, Washington

Each year, the National Hockey League tours many of the larger cities in the United States to promote the game of hockey, and often visits Seattle, Washington on the north-west coast of the USA. The famous Space Needle was designed for the 1962 World's Fair in Seattle. The fair's theme was 'Century 21', and the awe-inspiring Space Needle beautifully illustrated a modernistic approach to buildings. Originally called 'The Space Cage', the Space Needle was officially opened on April 21, 1962 – the first day of the World's Fair. Rising 605 feet (184.5 metres) from the ground to the tip of the aircraft warning beacon at the very top, there are 848 steps from the building's basement to the Observation Deck, from which the Stanley Cup was able to view Puget Sound, Mount Rainier and the skyscrapers of Seattle.

Travels With Stanley

WELCOME to the village of **White Fox**

Built By Families For Families

Population 445

Stanley Finds a Fox

White Fox, Saskatchewan

White Fox, Saskatchewan is comprised of just 465 residents, yet was selected as the site of CBC's first annual 'Hockey Day in Canada.' The tiny village is named after the beautiful white fox, often referred to as an Arctic fox, or, by its scientific name, alopex lagopus. The white fox is about the size of a pet cat with long, soft fur that changes colour with the season. To camouflage itself against the snow, it is a bright white in winter but in the spring and summer, the fur is grey. The white fox lives in burrows in bitter cold areas with plenty of rocks and snow, using its long, bushy tail like a scarf to wrap around itself while it sleeps. Although it will eat berries, insects and rodents, the white fox much prefers to follow polar bears and eat the remains of food left behind by the much larger mammal.

Stanley Enjoys a Reservation
Whitefish River, Ontario

First Nations is a term that refers to the descendants of indigenous peoples of Canada who are not of Inuit descent. Previous generations may have used the terms Indian, native Canadians or aboriginal peoples, although the Government of Canada officially uses the term 'registered Indians'. Treaties created predominantly during the 1800's isolated First Nations on reserves, which are lands specifically designated for First Nations. The Whitefish River reserve, for example, was identified in the Robinson-Huron Treaty of 1850 as a tract of land "contained between two rivers called White Fish River and Wanabitasebe, seven miles inland." Birch Island, found in Georgian Bay just east of Manitoulin Island, is home to the Whitefish River First Nation. The beauty of the area inspired regular visitor A.J. Casson of the world-renowned Group of Seven. U.S. President Franklin Roosevelt spent two weeks vacationing on Birch Island on his way to the Quebec Conference of 1943, where he discussed wartime strategy with Canadian Prime Minister Mackenzie King and British Prime Minister Winston Churchill. On a tour through the Manitoulin Islands, the Stanley Cup surprised the entire village, including Chief Shining Turtle, by visiting the Whitefish River Minor Hockey banquet.

Stanley Discovers Orr

Parry Sound, Ontario

Robert Gordon Orr was born March 20, 1948 in the Ontario town of Parry Sound. At the age of 14, he and his Dad Doug, were driven to Oshawa so Bobby could play for the Generals, the town's Junior 'A' team. By the time Bobby was 18, he was already starring for the Boston Bruins of the NHL. His career skyrocketed, with Orr accumulating an incredible array of silverware: two Stanley Cup championships, two Conn Smythe Trrophy wins as playoff MVP, the Calder Trophy as rookie of the year, the Hart Trophy recipient on three occasions, eight consecutive Norris Trophy wins as the NHL's best defenceman twice was recipient of the Art Ross Trophy as the league's top scorer, the Pearson Award winner in 1975, the Canada Cup MVP in 1976 and the Lester Patrick Trophy winner in 1979 for his contributions to hockey in the U.S. Sadly for hockey, knee injuries robbed Orr of much of his career, forcing him to retire during the 1978-79 season at the age of 29. The beautiful town of Parry Sound is a frequent stop for visitors to northern Ontario, and as the hometown of Bobby Orr, was a fitting place for the Stanley Cup to visit, too.

Travels With Stanley

Stanley Gets Beaver Fever

Beaver Lodge, Alberta

Look closely at the next Canadian nickel you find. There, you'll see a national symbol called a beaver. Not the Frank and Gordon beavers from the Bell commercials, but the second largest rodent after the capybara. Using their webbed feet and razor sharp incisors, the beaver increases the depth of pools by building dams out of branches and mud. This helps provide food and safety for their homes, called lodges, but can cause a great deal of damage to surrounding areas as often, the water level will rise too high and flood the neighbouring banks. The beaver is the national animal of Canada. In 2004, Jake Goertzen, the head scout of the Tampa Bay Lightning, split his day with the Stanley Cup between Fort St. John, British Columbia and Beaver Lodge, Alberta, the home of this monument.

Travels With Stanley

Stanley Has a Ball

Montclair, New Jersey

Just outside Montclair, New Jersey, the management of the New Jersey Devils shared the Stanley Cup with another of their favourite sports. People may 'love' the Stanley Cup, but as hard as it is to believe, that word is used even more often in the game of tennis. If you have not earned a point, your score is 'love.' It's an unusual term used in that way, but has a somewhat logical explanation. The number zero or nothing has a shape similar to an egg. The French word for 'the egg' is 'l'oeuf,' which sounds somewhat like 'love.' Strange but true, that's how the term 'love' began being used in tennis. Your serve!

Stanley, the Stars and Stripes

East Rutherford, New Jersey

A young widow who lost her husband in the Revolutionary War, Elizabeth 'Betsy' Ross operated an upholstery business in Philadelphia in 1776. It was there that she was approached by George Washington, who attended the same church as Betsy, to create a flag. General Washington sketched out his idea and Betsy went to work. She finished the flag in early June, 1776. The next month, the Declaration of Independence was read publicly for the first time and the Liberty Bell rang, announcing the birth of a nation. The flag consisted of thirteen stripes, one for each of the original thirteen colonies, with the stripes alternating red then white. In the upper left corner were thirteen white stars set in a circle, set upon a blue background, representing a new constellation. On a school visit with the New Jersey Devils, the players were thrilled to see this flag dedicated to the soldiers serving their country overseas.

Stanley Goes Down East

Fredericton, New Brunswick

Fredericton is one of Canada's oldest towns, and a town divided by its hockey loyalties. On a cross-Canada tour promoting the playoffs, the Stanley Cup discovered that half the town cheers for the Montreal Canadiens while the rest of the town is devoted to the Toronto Maple Leafs. Originally named Frederick's Town in honour of Prince Frederick Augustus, the Duke of York and son of King George III, the town's name was shortened to Fredericton shortly after it was named the official capital of New Brunswick in 1785.

Travels With Stanley

Stanley Hangs in Hockeytown
Detroit, Michigan

The Detroit River joins Lake St. Clair to Lake Erie. Because it is actually a body of water known as a 'strait,' it became known as the river of the strait, or in French, riviere du detroit. In 1701, the settlement that was built on its shores by the first settlers was called Fort Pontchartrain du Detroit. The French battled with the British, who overtook the settlement in 1760 and renamed it Detroit. The area was well-known as a fur-trading centre for years, later becoming the hub of the automobile industry when Henry Ford set up his shop there. In 2002, an estimated 500,000 fans descended on downtown Detroit for the Stanley Cup parade and celebration, proving that this huge metropolis truly is 'Hockeytown.'

Stanley Behind Bars

New York, New York

The New York Police Department had a little fun with the Stanley Cup, locking it up in jail to help raise funds for those families who lost loved ones in the 9/11 disaster. The Stanley Cup has never been involved in crime, but several people have tried to steal Lord Stanley's trophy through the years. During the playoffs in 1961-62, the Cup was on display in a glass case in the lobby of Chicago Stadium. A Montreal Canadiens fan by the name of Ken Kilander didn't like the fact that the Stanley Cup was being exhibited in Chicago, so he opened the case, reached in and grabbed the Cup. When no alarms began to ring, he walked through the lobby with the Cup, about to head outside. Just steps away from the exit door, a police officer noticed the man with the Stanley Cup. "Where do you think you're taking that," he was asked. Kilander's response?

"Back to Montreal where it belongs!"

Travels With Stanley

Stanley Views a Sunrise

York Harbor, Maine

The tranquil part of the morning when the sun first peeks over the horizon in the east is called the sunrise. Here, looking out over the Atlantic Ocean from York Harbor in Maine, the Stanley Cup rises early to observe the magnificent colours as the dawn of a new day is about to begin. It was David Conte, New Jersey's Director of Scouting, who woke up at his cottage with the Stanley Cup and this stunning view during the summer of 2003.

Stanley Watches Shinny

Montclair, New Jersey

Nobody really knows when hockey began. In the 1800's, various stick and ball
games evolved into the game we love today called hockey. Many towns and
cities lay claim to being the birthplace of hockey, but all that truly matters is
not who invented the game, but the fact that it is embraced by fans all around
the world. And although languages, cultures and uniforms may differ, the key
elements remain common to all – a stick, a puck, ice and a net. In Montclair,
New Jersey, families gather each weekend for a game of hockey, but this time
was even more special – the Stanley Cup was up for grabs!

Stanley On Top of the World
Mt. Elbert, Colorado

During the 1970's, John Denver introduced many of us to the beauty of Colorado in his song, 'Rocky Mountain High.' The state, named after the Rio Colorado ('red river,' due to its reddish-brown colour), enjoys an incredible array of land forms, from desert areas, to grasslands, to mountains. During the summer of 2001, several members of the staff of the Colorado Avalanche hiked up Mount Elbert with the Stanley Cup on their backs. Mount Elbert is not only the tallest mountain in the state, but is the highest peak in the Rocky Mountains located within the continental United States. Do you know how tall Mount Elbert is? Aww, you must have peaked (that's a mountain joke!) It's 4,400 metres (14,433 feet)!!

Stanley Reflects on Washington

Washington, D.C.

The Stanley Cup is gazing out over the Reflecting Pool, with the incredible Washington Monument in the distance. When the Washington Monument was officially opened in 1888, it was the tallest man-made structure in the world, standing 555 feet, 5 1/8 inches (169 metres) in height. The next year, the Eiffel Tower opened in France, making it the tallest structure. The Washington Monument was constructed of marble, granite and sandstone and is a United States Presidential Memorial created in honour of George Washington. During the 1998 Stanley Cup Final between Detroit and Washington, the Stanley Cup visited all the attractions in the U.S. capital before being taken over to the arena.

Travels With Stanley

Stanley Rides the Rails
Toronto, Ontario

Before British Columbia joined the Dominion of Canada in 1871, the newly-created province insisted that a transcontinental railway be built to link the easterly Canadian provinces to B.C. Between 1881 and 1885, thousands of dedicated workers carved a rail line through the forests, prairies and mountains to create this railway, and on November 7, 1885, Lord Strathcona drove the last spike of the Canadian Pacific Railway into the ties in Craigellachie, British Columbia. In 1978, VIA Rail Canada took over responsibility for the CPR's passenger service, although the VIA name wasn't used on the trains until the following year. Today, VIA serves 3.9 million passengers every year, traveling over 14,000 kilometres (8,700 miles) of track and serving 450 communities in Canada. The Stanley Cup was boarding a VIA train at Union Station in Toronto, headed for Ottawa and a fundraising event for the Senators.

Travels With Stanley

Stanley in the Hood

Elk River, Minnesota

The importance of civil safety is the prime motive of a police force. Although civilizations have long had people assigned to keep the peace, the first recognized police force was created in France in 1667. The London Metropolitan Police, established in the English capital in 1829, is regarded as the first modern police force, using their role to deter crime. Canada's first police force was founded in Toronto in 1834. The first police force in the United States was in Boston, founded in 1838. During every Stanley Cup celebration parade, the local police take part in some manner, often both officially and ceremonially.

Stanley in the Snow

Iqualit, Nunavut

On a tour of the Arctic Circle with Hockey Canada during the winter of 2003, the Stanley Cup witnessed a great deal of snow and ice in Iqualit, Nunavut. Adored by some and despised by others, there is an undeniable curiosity to ice and snow. In fact, several countries boast actual ice hotels. Although the idea originated in Sweden, every January since 2000, an ice hotel has been constructed in Sainte-Catherine-de-la-Jacques Cartier, located about 10 kilometres (just over 6 miles) from Quebec City. The Ice Hotel Quebec-Canada is open from January until the spring sunshine arrives in April. The hotel itself is created from 500 metric tons of ice (500,000 kilograms) and 15,000 metric tons (15 million kilograms) of snow and covers and area of 3,000 square metres (9,843 square feet). The walls of the hotel are four feet thick (1.22 metres), which works as an excellent insulator, keeping the temperature consistently between -2 to -5 degrees Celsius (28 to 23 degrees Fahrenheit). All the beds are made of ice but lined with deer fur and covered with mattresses and Arctic sleeping bags. All of the furniture is made from ice, too. Don't worry – the washrooms are located in a separate heated structure very close to the hotel!

Stanley Scans the Sea
Tampa, Florida

Although smaller than the Pacific, the Atlantic Ocean is an immense body of water covering approximately 20% of the earth's surface. The saltiest of the world's major oceans, the Atlantic is bounded on the west by North and South America and on the east by Europe and Africa. The early explorers sailed from Europe west in an attempt to find the route to China, and 'discovered' North and South America along the way. The deepest point within the Atlantic Ocean is Milwaukee Deep in the Puerto Rico Trench. That spot is 8,605 metres (28,232 feet) below the ocean's surface. Many members of the Tampa Bay Lightning took the Stanley Cup, as well as their families and friends, to the Atlantic coast during the summer of 2004.

Stanley Takes a Peak

Kamloops, British Columbia

Darryl Sydor of the Dallas Stars took the Stanley Cup home to Kamloops, British Columbia during the summer of 1999. The city of Kamloops is found in a fertile valley adjacent to British Columbia's Thompson River and nestled in amongst the Rocky Mountains. Because of its unique geography, Kamloops is a hotbed of sporting activities, including skiing and snowboarding, mountain biking, curling and, of course, hockey. Known as the Tournament Capital of Canada, Kamloops hosted the 1993 Canada Summer Games, the 2006 IIHF World Under-20 Hockey Championship and the 2006 B.C. Summer Games. The Stanley Cup has frequently traveled to Kamloops, and we wonder if nearby Pritchard and Campbell Creek were named after Cup Keepers Phil Pritchard and Craig Campbell?!?

Stanley Barbecues Reindeer

Pitea, Sweden

North Americans have to leave behind visions of Rudolph dancing in their heads and embrace a delicacy long-popular in Sweden. Guests sit inside sheds like this and enjoy a meal of reindeer over a traditional open barbecue. Reindeer meat is leaner than either beef or pork, and considered far more tender and tasty than either. And it is found in plentiful supply. Barbecue huts like this one allow the meat to cook slowly over an open fire, adding to the distinct and wonderful taste. Reindeer meat is often salted and dried, or made into sausages, too. In fact, every year, the Netherlands exports more and more of this exotic but delicious meat to North America, where it is finding a very dedicated marketplace. Any time the Stanley Cup travels to Sweden, it looks forward to a traditional Swedish barbecue. Roast reindeer with lingonberries – mmmm!

Stanley and the Silverware

Toronto, Ontario

It is often said that you can tell the quality of a place by its silverware. If that's the case, the Hockey Hall of Fame stands head and shoulders above the rest.

The home to the Stanley Cup, the Hockey Hall of Fame has other famous silverware, too! Pictured, you'll be able to see (clockwise, from top) the Prince of Wales Trophy for the Eastern Conference playoff champion, the Art Ross Trophy for the regular season scoring leader, the Lester B. Pearson Award for the most valuable performer in the regular season as voted on by the players, the Lady Byng Memorial Trophy for the league's most gentlemanly player, the Hart Memorial Trophy for the regular season's most valuable player as voted on by the Professional Hockey Writers' Association, the Conn Smythe Trophy for the playoff MVP and the Jack Adams Award for the NHL's top coach.

Stanley Goes for Gold
Montreal, Quebec

The ancient Olympic Games carried on every fourth year for almost 1,200 years before Roman emperor Theodosius abolished the competition because of its pagan influences. The Olympic Games were revived in 1896, and likes its predecessor, continues every four years. Women were first allowed to participate in the Olympic Games in 1900, and the Games were cancelled completely in 1916, 1940 and 1944 due to the World Wars raging at those times. Here, the Stanley Cup is proudly adorned with Marin Brodeur's gold medal, earned in Salt Lake City in 2002. The last time the Olympic gold medals were created entirely of gold was in 1912. Today, the gold medals are made of 92.5% silver, then covered in six grams of true gold.

Stanley Returns to His Place of Birth

London, England

After having been purchased in London, England in 1893, the Stanley Cup had not returned home until April 2006, when the local government designated the birthplace of the famous hockey trophy as a historic site. While in London, the Cup couldn't wait to go sightseeing, visiting many landmarks including the Tower Bridge. Although often mistakenly referred to as London Bridge, Tower Bridge has its own illustrious history. Two gigantic piers, containing more than 70,000 tons of concrete, were sunk deep into the bed of the River Thames to support the 11,000 tons of steel required to build the towers of the bridge. It took eight years to construct this magnificent span, and was opened in 1894 by the Prince of Wales, who later was crowned King Edward VII. Known as Tower Bridge because of its proximity to the Tower of London, this must-see landmark was at the centre of a near-disaster. Although traffic on the river is minimal compared to when the bridge opened, it still takes precedence over bridge traffic. In 1996, the motorcade carrying U.S. President Bill Clinton was stuck on Tower Bridge when the bridge unexpectedly opened for river traffic! Today, 24 hours' notice is needed before opening the bridge.

Stanley and the One that Got Away

Larder Lake, Ontario

Located 15 kilometres (just over 9 miles) from the Quebec border, the small community town of Larder Lake in Northern Ontario is rich with native history dating back close to 5,000 years. At one time, the town was home to fur traders, trading posts and lumber camps. Today, it is home to local forestry and mining operations. However, the most unique aspect of Larder Lake is that it is home to the world's largest fish monument, located beside the lake for which the town is named. At only three feet high (one metre), the Stanley Cup is dwarfed by the giant fish statue. On a trip heading north from Montreal to Hockey Heritage North in Kirkland Lake, Ontario, the Keepers of the Cup noticed the giant fish and couldn't resist a photograph

Stanley Sets the Stage

Nashville, Tennessee

What started out as a weekly barn dance on the fifth floor radio station almost 90 years ago has become a cultural phenomenon for country artists and fans around the world. Thousands of visitors each year visit Nashville, the home of country music, and every one of them makes certain that the Grand Ole Opry is a stop on their trip. Elvis Presley, Dolly Parton and Garth Brooks are just a few of the superstars to have graced the stage of the Grand Ole Opry. Today, fans of the Opry have more than one way to experience it — they can visit, listen on the radio or internet or watch on its weekly television show. While on a recent visit to Nashville for the Predators, the Stanley Cup made the short trip down the street to be on the Opry stage.

Travels With Stanley

ARCTIC

WATERSHED

ELEVATION   318 m

FROM HERE
ALL STREAMS
FLOW NORTH
INTO THE
ARCTIC OCEAN

Stanley at the Arctic Watershed

Matheson, Ontario

The landscape of Canada is vast and diverse, with a stunning array of urban centres, forests, lakes, rock and ice. But Canada also discharges 9% of the world's water supply and is home to one quarter of the world's wetlands. Due to the fact that the magnetic North Pole lies within the territory of Canada, at a certain point in Northern Ontario, the water begins to flow up instead of down river. While on a tour of Northern Ontario, the Stanley Cup stopped just outside Matheson, Ontario at an elevation of 318 metres (1,043 feet) above sea level — the exact spot where one side of the river flows north and the other side flows south.

Travels With Stanley

Stanley and the Stars

Dallas, Texas

The National Hockey League's mid-season classic is a who's who of the game's greatest players. A game that was initiated in the late 1940's has undergone numerous changes over the years, including the All-Star team playing the Stanley Cup champions, divisions vs. divisions and North America vs. the World. The annual NHL All-Star Game remains one of the NHL's great selling points.   In January 2006, the NHL took the All-Star contest to Dallas, Texas, where the Stanley Cup arrived on the back of a Harley Davidson motorcycle, much to the delight of hockey fans of all ages.

Stanley Takes a Backseat to No One

Kiev, Ukraine

Parades are held to celebrate special occasions, whether that is holidays (the Santa Claus Parade preceding Christmas, the Thanksgiving Day Parade, the Easter Parade) or just plain fun, like the Mardi Gras parade in New Orleans or the Orange Bowl Parade in Miami. The Stanley Cup parade is a traditional celebration, usually put together by the municipal government of the championship city. But any time the Stanley Cup is in town is reason enough to celebrate. The Stanley Cup is so revered that when it visits a city or town, it's a special occasion. This Stanley Cup party was with Anton Babchuk of the Carolina Hurricanes in Kiev, Ukraine during the summer of 2006.

Stanley and Baseball's Best

Boston, Massachusetts

Although they are brothers from different mothers, the championship trophy of hockey (the Stanley Cup) is pictured beside the championship trophy of baseball (the World Series Trophy). And even though they have much in common as the pinnacle of two major sports, there are a surprising number of differences. The Stanley Cup's actual name is the Dominion Hockey Challenge Cup. The World Series Trophy is officially known as the Commissioner's Trophy. The Stanley Cup is named after Lord Frederick Stanley, a Canadian Governor General. The World Series Trophy is the only major sports trophy not named after someone. The Stanley Cup, with its modifications through the years, has been passed down, each year, to the championship hockey team, while a new World Series Trophy is created each year and awarded to the winning World Series baseball team. The Stanley Cup has been awarded (with the exception of 1919 and 2005) every year since 1893. The World Series Trophy was first awarded in 2000. The Carolina Hurricanes' longtime equipment manager, Skip Cunningham, took the Stanley Cup to his hometown of Boston, Massachusetts during the summer of 2006, and couldn't resist heading over to Fenway Park to cheer on his beloved Red Sox.

Travels With Stanley

Stanley and the Statue
Kladno, Czech Republic

Backyards are the scene of many Stanley Cup parties. Each year, players from the winning Stanley Cup team have the opportunity to take the Cup back to their hometowns in order to celebrate with family and friends. Barbecues are often held, speeches made and toasts offered. All players celebrate in their own special way, a way unique to them. In Frantisek Kaberle's Czech Republic backyard stands a statue of a young hockey player pursuing the game he loves — perfectly suited to attend a Stanley Cup party for men who started the same way.

Stanley and Mr. Hockey®

Saskatoon, Saskatchewan

In 1998, The Hockey News rated Gordie Howe as the third greatest hockey player of all-time. On March 31, 1928, Gordie was born in Floral, Saskatchewan, a tiny village that has since been absorbed into Saskatoon. Floral is known for two things – a grain elevator built in 1927 that still stands today in the south-east corner of Saskatoon, and, of course, being the birthplace of the only person in hockey history to play NHL hockey during five decades – 1940's through 1980's. At the time of his retirement, including NHL, WHA and playoffs in both leagues, Howe had played 2,421 games, scored 1,071 goals, contributed 1,518 assists and collected 2,589 points. The Stanley Cup, which Gordie won four times during his career, is pictured beside a statue of Howe in downtown Saskatoon, which since this picture, has been relocated to Saskatoon's Credit Union Sports and Entertainment Centre.

Travels With Stanley

Stanley Camps Out
Montreal, Quebec

During Martin Brodeur's three Stanley Cup celebrations, the Stanley Cup was taken to his summer home in Quebec where during late-night bonfires, his children used the bowl of the historic hockey trophy to hold marshmallows for roasting. Real marsh mallows are plants found primarily in Europe that sport long, spongy roots. Although dating back to ancient Egypt, this medicinal candy was popularized in the mid-1800's when the sap from these marshy roots was extracted and cooked with egg whites and sugar, then whipped into a meringue that was allowed to harden. The resulting 'candy' was then used by doctors to treat children with sore throats. Marshmallows are not used for healing scratchy throats today, nor is the mallow plant used to manufacture the treat. Instead, as Anthony, twins Jeremy and William, and Anabelle Brodeur discovered, roasting marshmallows, whether the Cup is involved or not, is just about the greatest campfire treat in the world.